POMPEII

Karen Ball

Illustrated by Emmanuel Cerisier

History consultant: Dr. Anne Millard

Reading consultant: Alison Kelly
Roehampton University

Internet links

For links to websites where you can find out more about Pompeii, go to the **Usborne Quicklinks Website** at **www.usborne-quicklinks.com** and type the keywords "**yr pompeii**".
The recommended websites are regularly reviewed and updated but, please note, Usborne Publishing is not responsible for the content of websites other than its own.

Edited by Jane Chisholm
Designed by Andrea Slane
Cover design by Laura Fearn

Acknowledgements
© CORBIS pages 53, 54-55, 55, 58-59, 60, 61
© AKG page 60 (ml)

First published in 2006 by Usborne Publishing Ltd.,
Usborne House, 83-85 Saffron Hill,
London ECIN 8RT, England.
www.usborne.com

Printed in China
First published in America in 2006.

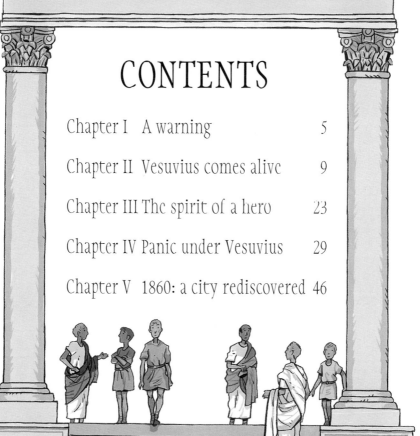

CONTENTS

Map

ITALY

Pompeii

SICILY

to Rome

ITALY

Naples

Misenum

Mt. Vesuvius

Herculaneum

Pompeii

Pliny's route

Mediterranean Sea

CAPRI

CHAPTER 1
A warning

February 5 AD79

It was a cold February morning when
the people of Pompeii were woken by a
dull rumble. Dogs suddenly leapt to their
feet and began barking in the street.

5

At the baths, the surface of the water trembled – even though there were no bathers there at this hour to disturb it.

As people clambered out of their beds, half asleep and confused, several sharp cracks rang out, as if a slave were breaking up stones. But it was too early for anyone to be working. One or two people ran to their doors and saw that the Temple of the Capitoline Triad had been damaged. Stones lay in a pile of rubble on the ground.

At least no one's been hurt!

One of the statues had lost its head and
a few of the central columns had long,
angry cracks
running down
the middle.

And when the local baker, Terentius, returned home, he noticed that his oven had been damaged. The wreckage was everywhere. What had caused it?

An earthquake. But Pompeii was used to regular earth tremors. So no one thought much more about it.

The birds began singing again and people returned to the warmth of their beds. After all, no one had been hurt.

Not yet...

CHAPTER II

Vesuvius comes alive

August 24 AD79

The morning started furiously hot – even
hotter than a normal August day – but
Pompeii's market traders wasted no time
setting up their stalls in the Forum. No
one spared a glance for the Temple of the
Capitoline Triad. Repaired by stonemasons
months ago, most people had forgotten it
had ever been damaged.

From under the
shade of a leafy plane tree,
a few curious citizens looked
on as a wealthy lady paraded
through the square in the comfort
of her carrying chair, with her slaves
in attendance.

She gazed at the traders
busy preparing for a day of good
business, as they laid out their wares
under the watchful eye of a statue of
Mercury, the god of commerce.

A shoemaker put out his tools and wine merchants lined up their flagons. Fabric, pottery, wool, bread, honey – thanks to the ships that came to the nearby port of Puteoli, everything was on sale here, as long as the browsers had a few coins in their pockets.

No one noticed that the Sun was looking unusually hazy in the sky. By ten o'clock, the market was in full swing. Traders called out their wares, slaves wandered from stall to stall, buying everything on the day's shopping list.

In a corner, an old man with a stoop was busily adding his own graffiti to Pompeii's local notice board – a city wall. With no telephones or postal service, this was the way most people in Pompeii left messages for each other.

But this man wasn't happy with what he saw on the wall and he decided to say so:

Oh, wall! I can't believe you haven't fallen down under the weight of all these boring messages!

He rubbed his hands in satisfaction and turned away. But then his chisel slipped and fell with a clatter to the ground.

His eyes were fixed on the horizon as he raised a limp finger to point at what he saw. A blind beggar brushed past him, looking for a few spare coins, and walked into his outstretched arm.

"Give me half a chance, mate. What are you doing, sticking your arm out like that? Could cause an injury!"

But the old man didn't reply. So the beggar moved on, frustrated, still rattling his alms plate.

Finally, the man seemed to come to his senses, shouting frantically to the people around him. Passers-by looked around over their shoulders – until they realized what he was pointing at.

Gasps and nervous laughs filled the air. No one heard what the man said next. "Look! The volcano is stirring!" Then he backed away, not looking behind him, his eyes glued to the thin column of smoke coming out of the top of Mount Vesuvius.

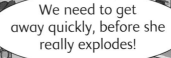

He looked desperately at the people jostling next to him. But people just shook their heads and turned their backs. Slowly, he understood that no one was really listening to him. The people of Pompeii were used to the occasional flurry of activity from Vesuvius.

Why's he shouting?

Only the old man thought
of the earthquake a few months
ago and made a connection
between the two events.
Everyone else just smiled,
wondering what the gods were upset
about this time – and turned back to
their business.

In his haste to get
away, the man stumbled
into one of the open
aqueducts and kicked his
way up the stream of
water. As he ran, a large
flake of ash fell onto
his tunic, as softly as
a flake of snow.
He brushed it away,
leaving a dark smear
across the pale linen.

When he reached his home in
the Via delle Terme, he found his
wife sitting next to the fountain in
their walled garden.

He pulled her roughly to her feet and
shouted at her to prepare to leave.

"But where are we going?" she asked.

"Away from that!" he shouted back, his finger pointing at Mount Vesuvius in the background. Without a word, his wife hurried indoors.

An hour later they were hurrying down the street towards one of the city gates, the Herculaneum Gate. From a doorway, a woman was calling her children to come inside. She shook her head as they passed.

"We're taking shelter," she called out. "With luck, we can sit this one out."

"I wouldn't be so sure," muttered the man under his breath. But he'd always been known for his terrible predictions. No one except his wife ever believed they would come true.

Come here, children!

CHAPTER III

The spirit of a hero

Not everyone was so concerned for their
safety. Across the bay from Pompeii, Pliny
the Elder – scholar and admiral of the fleet
at Misenum – stood at the window of his
house. He pulled his cloak tighter around
his shoulders. In the distance he could see
a column of smoke emerging from Mount
Vesuvius, high above sea level.

23

With each passing hour, the plume of smoke streaming out of the volcano had become larger and more ominous.

This hadn't prevented him from keeping to his usual routine: a cold bath followed by a light lunch of bread, figs, and olives, sitting beneath the mural of Venus of the Shell on the dining room wall. Even his nephew, Pliny the Younger, seemed happy to continue calmly with his studies.

Eventually, a slave came into the room to clear away the lunch things. Without turning from the window, Pliny gave him an order: "Get a ship ready for me. Right away, please."

He continued gazing at the smoke that was now hanging over the town like a cloud.

"Out into the bay. I want to get a closer look."

The slave hesitated, wondering if he was brave enough to question his master.

"Are you sure?" he asked. Pliny turned from the window. With the light behind him, it was impossible for the slave to make out the expression on his master's face. He could not see the animated glint in the old man's eye that indicated neither fear nor dread. Pliny only felt excitement.

"Of course I'm sure."

Pliny emerged from the house, followed by a small group. Suddenly his sister ran out of the house and broke through the crowd to bar his way.

"Don't try to stop me," he said gently.

"No, no. This came for you," she panted, thrusting a rolled up papyrus message into his hand. Looking at his sister suspiciously, Pliny the Elder unfurled the papyrus and carefully read its contents:

Help! Send a boat for me!
Can you see it? Vesuvius is exploding and pumice stones are raining down on us.
I need to get away!
Your friend Rectina.

"A change of plan," muttered Pliny, still studying the note. His sister let out a sigh of relief.

"Thank goodness you've come to your senses, I was so worried about you."

But he ignored his sister and looked up at the captain who had been waiting patiently for his orders.

Carry me to Rectina's house.

"Fortune befriends the brave: we'll set sail right away."

Only Pliny could see the nervous twitch that had started up in the captain's eye.

"Where are we going?" asked the captain.

"To Pompeii, of course!"

No one dared suggest Pliny abandon his plan. No one wanted to look like a coward. It was time for action.

Led by Pliny the Elder, a group of men walked purposefully towards the jetty where the ships were waiting to take them right into the shadow of Vesuvius. As they climbed aboard, trying not to look down at the water below them, only a few of the men noticed the unusually choppy sea.

Pliny the Younger and his mother stood at the edge of the jetty, holding on to each other and waving as Pliny the Elder set sail towards danger. They did not know that they would never see him again.

CHAPTER IV
Panic under Vesuvius

At six o'clock in the evening, Pliny arrived at the house of his old friend Pomponianus. This was a good place to rest before sailing on to help Rectina and any others to escape. As he settled down for a good night's sleep, the foundations of the house shook badly. Outside, pumice stones fell on the heads of anyone who dared step out for a better look.

"Don't panic," Pliny reassured Pomponianus. "If you must go outside, tie a pillow on your head with a napkin."

"Are you sure we shouldn't go and get Rectina right away?" asked his friend uncertainly, as he watched the leaping flames of fire light up the night sky at several points on Mount Vesuvius. The day was drawing to a close, but none of the heat had waned.

"I need to rest first," explained Pliny, as he shut his bedroom door.

Pomponianus turned away from the door and bit his lip anxiously, wondering whether or not to risk running out to give the pigs a last feed for the day.

Neither of them knew how much panic was brewing among the 20,000 people who lived in the city, only a few miles away.

As midnight approached, people poured through the gates of Pompeii. The heat was appalling and people wandered around with cuts and bruises on their faces from the falling pumice stones. Ash lay like a soft carpet over everything. It was difficult to do anything without becoming smeared in black soot. Cracks were appearing in the corners of buildings as the ground shook.

Run, run, as fast as you can...

At the Herculaneum Gate, a woman stood with her baby in her arms and her two small girls clinging onto the skirts of her toga. Her cries went unanswered.

The children cried as the woman's eyes desperately searched the hordes of people for her husband. They had become separated in the crowd.

Did she dare wait for him any longer?

Or should she rush on to the Bay of Naples with their children, hoping that someone would find space for four extra passengers on a boat away from the city?

At the Nucerian Gate, a beggar carrying a sack called out desperately for help. His limp meant he would never be able to walk quickly enough to make a decent escape if Vesuvius erupted.

And Vesuvius looked angry.

Won't anyone take pity on me? I can't escape on my own!

Some people didn't have any possibility of escape – it was their duty to stay put. In the gladiators' barracks, 60 gladiators tried to settle down to sleep. But it was difficult in the heat and the noise.

One of them, Actius Anicetus, lay on his back in his bed and held out a hand in front of his face. He watched his fingers tremble and wondered if he'd ever see dawn break. Gladiators shouldn't feel scared. He'd fought in the amphitheatre, hadn't he? But he had to be brave.

Actius concentrated on stopping the trembling that shook his body. For a long time sleep evaded him, until finally his muscles relaxed and he closed his eyes.

He was woken suddenly at midnight by a noise that seemed to tear the sky apart. He felt it first as a rumble, vibrating through the frame of his bed, then he was thrown rudely to the floor by the shifting of the building. The tiles on the roof were smoking, as hot rocks hit them. Actius ran outside, sure that the barracks were about to collapse.

May the gods help me!

His way was blocked by deep drifts of ash. He looked down at his feet, hidden in the soft, warm piles of ash and wondered how so much could have happened in the few hours that he'd been asleep. He didn't know that a burning cloud of ash had been falling on his city all through the night.

The night sky throbbed with the orange glow of fire. But it wasn't the familiar crackle of flames that lit up the midnight scene. There was another source of light and heat – closer to the ground. Racing down the side of Vesuvius, Actius could see the steady flow of molten rocks, moving towards the city with a deadly speed of 35km (20 miles) an hour.

He instinctively gasped in shock and immediately regretted it. Now his throat was burned dry by the raging heat and toxic gases. He clutched his neck and closed his mouth, desperately trying to breathe through his nose.

Actius struggled to get enough air – but
every breath filled his lungs with poison.
Feeling dread and panic in the pit of his
stomach, he knew that any bravery
he once had had finally
deserted him.

All around him rang out the sounds of panic. As Actius began to run through the streets of Pompeii, there were too many disturbing scenes to take in.

A child lay in the street, as if asleep. Actius rushed past. He could see the deadly blow to the young boy's head and the large molten rock that lay next to him. The edges of the boy's tunic were scorched from the large flakes of ash that had been falling on him.

Close by, a dog chained to a building pulled on his chain in a frenzy – unable to escape but aware of the heat and danger. All around, cries of desperation rang in Actius' ears. There was nothing he could do.

A couple emerged from a building. Actius recognized them as Terentius Neo, the baker, and his wife. In her arms she still grasped the writing tablets she used to keep their accounts. They held their hands out to Actius, begging him to help them carry their belongings out of their villa.

Drop everything and run!

But the gladiator had no time to stop.

"Get to the coast," he shouted, as he pushed past, pulling himself free of the grasp of their fingers at his cloak. "It's your only hope."

Then, with a small nod, they joined the rush of people all heading for the same place – the Marine Gate. As they crowded around the bay, a few even fell into the water, as the crowd surged behind them.

41

Slaves, gentlewomen, farmers, traders, scholars, gladiators – everyone was thrown together in the panic to escape. But escape to where? Desperately, people began to throw themselves into the water, hoping it might save them from the heat. But how could they breathe in the thick smoke?

Out in the bay, Actius could just make out Pliny the Elder at the helm of a ship. Everyone in Pompeii knew and recognized Pliny, the admiral of the fleet. He had several evacuees aboard ship with him. They were in a state of panic, pointing in the direction of the city and screaming and shouting.

The ship was slowly turning around, away from Vesuvius. Actius prayed to the gods that Pliny and his crew would escape the devastation. Then Actius looked behind him towards where the people were pointing, at the city of Pompeii – the city that he had loved and been proud of.

He saw that the buildings were being submerged in ash and torrents of mud. Soon the river of mud and deadly piles of ash would reach him too.

Actius opened his mouth and took in a deep breath of air. It felt as though his lungs were burning and the pain was almost unbearable. Bracing himself, he took another deep breath, and saw Pompeii turn blurry as his vision began to fail him. Another gulp of air made him sink to his knees. It was with a sigh of relief that he softly collapsed on the ground.

His helmet and dagger were no good to him now. It wasn't how the brave gladiator had imagined death. For the second time that night, he closed his eyes.

CHAPTER V

1860: a city rediscovered

For centuries after the disaster, Pompeii lay buried and forgotten, hidden under layers of dust, dirt and rubble. Occasionally a farmer digging his field would turn up a small fragment of mosaic or sculpture, or a piece of bronze – but nothing more.

Then, in 1748, whispers began to spread that the ruins of some very ancient houses had been dug up by local workmen. Word soon reached the ears of the King and Queen of Naples. Intrigued, they ordered excavations to begin.

Over the next hundred years, all sorts of treasures were discovered and entire buildings began to rise from the ashes. Pompeii became famous as a popular tourist hotspot. Everyone flocked to see the site – not just scholars and archaeologists, but rich young Europeans touring Italy to put the finishing touches to their education.

The excavations were often chaotic and slow. Some excavators made detailed drawings and studies of what they found. But others just grabbed what they could for their private collections. But all that was soon to change...

One morning in 1860, the voice of a workman rang out excitedly. He'd spent hours on his knees, sifting carefully through layers of debris, under the instruction of the inspiring new Director of Excavations, Giuseppe Fiorelli.

Director!
Over here!

Giuseppe Fiorelli was young, dedicated and ambitious. The Italian king, Victor-Emmanuel II, knew he had found the right man for the job. For too long, this forgotten city had been plundered by amateurs wanting to take away their very own piece of history. It was time to show Pompeii the respect it deserved.

With over 500 workmen at his disposal,
Fiorelli was determined to do just that.

He walked over for a closer look,
pushing his panama hat further back on
his head. They peered at a small hole in
the earth that indicated another cavity
containing ... who knew what? Fiorelli
nodded and clapped his hand on the
workman's shoulder.

Fiorelli walked towards the top of a small hillock to assess the day's work and to admire the slowly emerging city. He leaned against an olive tree and watched as a line of men with wicker baskets on their backs carried rubble away from the site. Others stood on wooden scaffolding as they removed the debris that had submerged the houses of Pompeii. They worked from the roof down, so as not to disturb any relics.

On one of the far houses, a wall painting had been slowly appearing over the past few days, and Fiorelli felt a flush of excitement.

Meanwhile, Luigi poured his freshly mixed plaster into the small opening in the earth, sitting back on his haunches as the last of the plaster dripped from the bucket into the cavity.

It would take some time to set. So he stood up and stretched his aching limbs. He might only have been a humble workman, but Luigi was almost as excited as Fiorelli. After all, he'd seen what had already been discovered using this brand new technique.

He didn't like to say it out loud, but Luigi thought Fiorelli was a genius. As the excavation had continued, everyone commented on the cavities that kept emerging and then collapsing as the workmen sifted through the ash from that long-ago eruption. It soon became clear that these holes contained the shapes of long-disintegrated bodies, captured by the volcanic ash.

Fiorelli was determined to recapture them. So he'd invented a technique of pouring plaster into the cavity through a small hole. When the plaster set inside the cavity, it could be dug out.

In this way they had already recovered the contorted body of a dog, a girl covering her face with a tunic, and a man trying to climb out of a window. The detail was incredible – down to the pattern of a fabric or individual hairs on a person's head. They were a part of history that had been frozen forever.

Which new character would emerge this time?

This is the plaster cast of a chained-up dog in his death throes, found at Pompeii. You can still see the thick collar around his neck.

Luigi slung his bucket over his shoulder and walked towards the tent where a simple lunch was waiting.

The next day, Fiorelli and Luigi met at the same spot and peered at the ground.

"It's set, I'm sure," said Luigi.

"Let's start, then," agreed Fiorelli. The two of them knelt on the ground and started to clear away the ash and earth around their new plaster cast. It was slow and dirty work, but they knew it would be worth it. By mid-morning, the details of this new personality were emerging.

"It's a gladiator. We've not had many of them," said Fiorelli.

"Look. You can tell from the dagger he's holding. Only men trained in the Capuan schools were allowed to use them."

Gladiators' helmets, like this one found at Pompeii, were highly decorative, as well as protecting the face from swords.

As they continued digging, they could see that their gladiator had died with his knees flexed and forearms raised. Fiorelli pointed at the gladiator's clenched fists.

"It's typical. Look at the way he holds his body in death."

"What do you mean?"

Bodies like this were found all over Pompeii. Fiorelli's casts show their position the moment they were buried by lava and ash.

"It's the muscles. They contract in extremely high temperatures.
Any body retrieved from a burning building, even today, will look the same."

"Do you think he suffered?" asked Luigi. Fiorelli tipped his head to one side as he looked at the body.

"He probably suffocated. So he would have been unconscious by the time the ash and molten rocks got to him."

"Still, it's a grim death," murmured Luigi as the two of them stood up again.

"But what a place in history! Immortality! I'm sure a gladiator would have liked that."

The two men bowed their heads as they surveyed the shape of a man who had walked the streets of Pompeii so many hundreds of years before them. This was a gladiator who had slept in a barracks, fought at the Games of Apollo, and bathed in the Temple baths.

"To be a citizen of Pompeii," said Fiorelli quietly. "That was something to be really proud of."

The two men walked away in the fading light. The sea lapped gently in the bay and the leaves of the trees rustled gently in the breeze. All was calm as the workmen downed their tools and set off for home.

In the distance, Mount Vesuvius watched over the scene as another day drew to a close. It had been another day in the life of Pompeii – a city that would never die.

This is how Pompeii looks today.

Archaeologists have been hard at work at Pompeii ever since Fiorelli's time, and every year, thousands of visitors flock to see the treasures they have discovered.

Treasures of Pompeii

Here are just some of the amazing things archaeologists have discovered at Pompeii.

This engraving of 1776 shows the Temple of Isis during excavations from 1764-1765.

This fossilized loaf of bread was found in the ruins of a bakery.

A mosaic of a family dog was found in one of the houses in Pompeii.

This mosaic found in the House of the Faun shows Alexander the Great, the ruler of the Greek empire.

The Roman goddess Venus appears in a wall painting in the House of the Venus Marina.

In this wall painting, the baker Terentius Neo and his wife are dressed in their finest clothes.

Here are some of the glass dishes and jewels found in the ruins of Pompeii.

The gold charm on the right, called a *bulla*, was for a child. It came from the House of the Menander.

Plan of Pompeii

This plan of Pompeii shows many of the places mentioned in the story, as well as important sites – villas, temples, theatres, amphitheatres and baths – that have been discovered by archaeologists. You can find out when they were excavated in the timeline on page 64.

Vesuvius Gate

Herculaneum Gate

Marine Gate

1 Villa of the Mysteries

2 Villa of Diomedes

3 House of the Vettii

4 House of the Faun

5 House of the Silver Wedding

6 Central Baths

7 Via delle Terme
(where the old man lived)

8 Forum Baths

Nucerian
Gate

POMPEII TIMELINE

AD79   Mount Vesuvius erupts and Pompeii and Herculaneum are destroyed. Of the 20,000 people at Pompeii, about 2,000 die.

104   Pliny the Younger (nephew of Pliny the Elder) writes an account of the destruction of Pompeii.

1748   The first systematic excavations begin at Pompeii.

1762   A German scholar named Johann Winckelmann writes about the discoveries at Pompeii and Herculaneum. This starts a European craze for the 'Pompeii style' in fashions and interior design.

1763   A tomb with the name of Pompeii inscribed on it is discovered. This clearly establishes the city's identity for the first time.

1764–65   A theatre, an amphitheatre and the Temple of Isis are excavated.

1771   The Villa of Diomedes is excavated, containing the bodies of 18 women and children huddled together.

1812   Excavations begin in the Forum.

1830–32   The House of the Faun is first excavated.

1860   Giuseppe Fiorelli is appointed director of excavations at Pompeii. He introduces his technique of making plaster casts in **1862**.

1868   The House of the Citharist is excavated.

1893   The House of the Silver Wedding is excavated.

1894–95   The House of the Vettii, with spectacular wall paintings, is excavated.

1895   Roman silver tableware, known as the Boscoreale Treasure, is found.

1924–61   Amedeo Maiuri leads excavations at Pompeii. Many important discoveries are made, including the House of the Menander, which contains a hoard of silver treasure and gold jewels (**1927–32**), the Villa of the Mysteries, one of Pompeii's oldest and grandest houses (**1929–30**), and the Palaestra, the sports ground (**1938–39**).

1944   Vesuvius erupts again – the latest of about 36 eruptions since AD**79**.

1997   Pompeii is listed as a UNESCO World Heritage Site.

2005   A magnificent silver 20-piece dinner service is put on show. It was discovered in **2000** during road-building work just outside Pompeii.